What NOT to Do in Polite Company!

What NOT to Do in Polite Company!
Copyright © 2005 Sweetwater Press
Produced by Cliff Road Books

Printed in The United States of America

ISBN: 1-58173-405-0

This work is a compilation from numerous sources. Every effort has been made to ensure accuracy. However, the publisher cannot be responsible for incorrect information.

What NOT to Do in Polite Company!

Compiled and Edited by
Linda J. Beam

SWEET WATER PRESS

About the Author

Linda J. Beam holds a B.A. in English from Judson College, and an M.A. in English from the University of Alabama at Birmingham. Her extensive editorial experience includes work with medical journals and textbooks, and a variety of corporate publications. In addition, she has developed and presented business communication seminars on business writing, and basic grammar and punctuation. She currently works as Managing Editor at Crane Hill Publishers in Birmingham, Alabama. Her other works include *What NOT to Say!*, *What NOT to Name Your Baby!*, and *What's Your Bible I.Q.?*.

Contents

Things Emily Post Didn't Have to Deal With

Good manners are important in every aspect of our lives. They help create good personal and professional relationships, give us confidence to deal with social situations, and provide guidelines for treating others properly and respectfully.

People have always been interested in the courtesies of living and working together. As early as 2500 BC, Ptahhotep's scroll advised young Egyptian men on the fast track, "When sitting with one's superior, laugh when he laughs." The first American book on etiquette was written by none other than George Washington, who produced his Rules of Civility at the ripe old age of sixteen. Without question the most popular work has been Emily Post's 1923 landmark volume that called attention again to our behavior, and offered advice on how to conduct oneself in almost any imaginable situation.

But let's face it: the famous manners maven lived and wrote in a simpler era when children were seen and not heard, and when even close acquaintances were addressed by formal titles like Mr. and Mrs. She didn't have to tolerate rude cell phone users or worry about sending a proper e-mail. Yes, the particulars of our society have changed, but one thing that remains constant is the need for considerate behavior. In fact, it is because life is so fast-paced and complex that we appreciate more than ever courtesies that make our lives gentler and kinder.

This book addresses how we can apply kindness and consideration to the issues that are truly signs of our times: electronic communication, mixing muscles and manners at the gym, and even dating. Also included are guidelines to help with the big occasions in life that have always posed etiquette dilemmas: births, weddings, and funerals. Above all, it reminds us that the best etiquette is really based on common sense, and the ultimate goal is to make others feel comfortable no matter the situation.

Baby Basics: Booties, Bibs, and Behavior

Baby Basics:
Booties, Bibs, and Behavior

*I*s there anything more exciting than a new baby! Don't let all the fun of waiting for and welcoming the new addition make you forget the basics of good behavior. Here are some ways to make this time extra special for the new family.

BABY SHOWERS

A baby shower is an exciting time for the mom-to-be. Make it one she will always remember by observing the simple courtesies provided below.

What NOT to Do

- Do not have the shower too close to the baby's due date in case he or she makes an early appearance.

- Do not pay attention to old rules about who may plan the shower. Nowadays, even close relatives may host the event.

- Do not issue invitations without checking with the mom-to-be about the guest list.

- Do not forget to let guests know where the prospective parents are registered for gifts.

- Do not plan to play games that might embarrass the mom-to-be if the shower will be co-ed, like games that focus on the expectant mom's tummy.

- Do not skimp on quantities of food; have extra on hand.

> **"Courtesies of a small and trivial character are the ones which strike deepest in the grateful and appreciating heart."**
> Henry Clay

- Do not include alcohol in the refreshments unless the mom-to-be approves.

- Do not expect perfection. Be prepared if problems arise, and realize that you can't control everything.

What to Do

- Plan the shower for a month or two before the due date.

- Take the wishes of the mom-to-be into account. Ask her opinion about the guest list, games, and all other details for the occasion.

- Ask the mom-to-be for preferences about the food since there may be some off-limits to her because of health reasons, or that she can't tolerate during her pregnancy.

- Send written shower invitations with the date and other pertinent information such as location and directions so guests will have all the details they need at their fingertips.

- Consider sending less frilly invitations if the party will be co-ed.

> **Shower gifts need not be expensive to be appreciated. Coupons for baby sitting and house cleaning are always welcomed.**

- Invite guests by phone if there is not time to mail invitations. Try to give as much notice as possible.

- Provide a contact number for guests to call if they have questions about the arrangements.

- Start the shower on time and keep it fairly short.

- Greet guests at the door as they arrive, and walk them to the door as they leave.

- Open gifts while all guests are there, just in case some have to leave early.

- Hand gifts to the mom-to-be to open, and take them from her once she's done. This will save her the inconvenience of continually getting up and down to pick up gifts.

- Be sensitive to the energy level of the mom-to-be and be alert to signs of her fatigue.

- Include dad by buying him a special gift. If the new baby will have older siblings, it is also good to include small gifts for each of them so they won't feel left out.

- Record each gift so the mom-to-be can send a thank-you note to each gift giver.

- Be sure to thank guests for coming.

CELEBRATING THE NEW ADDITION

New babies are irresistible, which makes everyone want to visit and hold them. But many new moms feel that good manners go out the window when people come to see the new darling. Know how to be a welcomed guest by following these suggestions for celebrating the new family member.

What NOT to Do

- Do not visit the newborn until you are sure the mother feels like having company.

Baby Basics:
Booties, Bibs, and Behavior

- Do not visit without calling first.

- Do not ask to visit at critical times during the day, such as when dad gets home from work or near mealtime.

- Do not expect to be entertained and fed when visiting a new mother.

- Do not pick up the baby unless the mom offers. You might ask for permission, but she probably would say "Yes" to be polite even if she would rather say "No."

- Do not ask if your young child may hold the baby.

- Do not offer unsolicited advice on how to bring up the baby.

- Do not visit a new baby if you or anyone in your family has had a cold or flu.

What to Do

- Call ahead before you visit.

- Ask the new parents when the best time to visit will be.

- Allow the mother and baby's wellbeing to be the top priority.

- Respect the parents' wishes if they request no visitors.

- Treat the baby as an individual by calling him or her by name.

- Smile – the baby will respond.

- Talk to the baby in complete sentences. Use baby talk sparingly.

- Keep visits short.

- Offer to bring a snack tray or a casserole for the family's dinner.

- Allow privacy when the new mother indicates that she is breastfeeding.

- Pay attention to the new baby's siblings when you visit. A small gift can let them know they are still special.

MISCARRIAGE/LOSS OF AN INFANT

Few situations are more difficult to manage than the loss of a child. There is nothing anyone can do to change the circumstances, but there are some ways you can help grieving parents get through the situation.

What NOT to Do

- Do not make comments to minimize the loss. Phrases to avoid include the following:

> "You'll get over it in time."
> "You can always have other children."
> "It was nature's way of taking care of a problem."
> "You already have other children."
> "It was probably for the best.
> "At least you were only a few weeks along."

The Miscarriage Association provides support and information for those who have experienced the loss of a pregnancy. A network of volunteers who have had similar experiences offers support, understanding, and a listening ear.

Baby Basics:
Booties, Bibs, and Behavior

- Do not say "I know how you feel" unless you have experienced the same kind of loss and really do know how it feels.

- Do not compare the loss to someone else's by saying, "I know someone who…."

- Do not avoid talking about the child. Mention his or her name and allow parents to talk about the plans they had for the child. Continue to talk about the child even as time passes.

- Do not offer advice about how to deal with the loss.

- Do not ask grieving parents how they are doing unless you are interested in their honest answer.

- Do not expect grief to follow a set course. Everyone experiences grief differently.

- Do not forget to offer support to siblings of the child, or extended family members like grandparents.

- Do not try to rush the grieving process. It will take time.

- Do not try to explain the loss.

- Do not criticize feelings of anger or disappointment expressed by the parents.

- Do not underestimate the loss that the dad feels. Although he did not carry the child or give birth, he has still lost a child.

What to Do
- Offer sincere expressions of sympathy, such as, "I am sorry for your loss," or "I am here for you."

Baby Basics:
Booties, Bibs, and Behavior

- Acknowledge that the baby existed by talking about him or her.

- Stay available to just listen. Sometimes it's best to say nothing at all.

- Allow the grieving parents to talk about the loss.

- Remain patient. There is no standard time for grief to run its course.

- Offer to keep baby items or other memorabilia until the family is ready to see them.

- Ask if you may be of help in planning a memorial service.

- Encourage the parents to attend a support group.

- Be tolerant of unpredictable emotional responses.

- Be aware that family and friends dealing with miscarriage or the loss of an infant may not want to hear about other pregnancies or new babies.

- Keep in touch with the family not just for the days after the loss, but for the weeks and months to follow.

- Remember the family during difficult times such as the anniversary of the baby's due date.

Business Etiquette: Minding Your Own Business

Business Etiquette:
Minding Your Own Business

*K*nowing *how to behave appropriately in business
situations is not just a "soft skill" that is nice to have.
On the contrary, the mastery of business etiquette is
something employers expect. Make sure you know how to
conduct yourself in business settings by observing the
guidelines offered below.*

INTERVIEWING

The first step of your entry into the business world will be interviewing
for the job you want. The first impression you make will no doubt be
the one that stands out in the mind of a future employer, so you want
your initial meeting to be perfect. Be careful about the following
things to help land the job you want!

What NOT to Do
- Do not eat strong foods before your interview. The lingering aroma
  of garlic and onion can undermine an otherwise good first
  impression.

> **People do bizarre things in interviews: one
> interviewer reported a candidate that ate a
> hamburger and French fries, then wiped up the
> ketchup with her sleeve while talking with a
> potential employer. Another job seeker paused
> from an interview long enough to phone his
> psychiatrist for advice on answering questions
> posed to him.**

Business Etiquette:
Minding Your Own Business

- Do not call the company fifteen minutes before your interview to frantically ask for directions.

- Do not be late! Arrive ten minutes early. This will give you time to calm yourself.

- Do not arrive too early and loiter in the lobby or reception area.

> ## "You never get a second chance to make a good first impression."
> Unknown

- Do not answer your cell phone during an interview. Your phone should be turned off.

- Do not smoke, eat, or chew gum during an interview. You may accept a cup of coffee or a soft drink if offered.

- Do not forget that first impressions count with everyone. Be courteous to the parking attendant, the security guard, and the receptionist.

- Do not discuss your personal life during the interview.

- Do not make jokes or remarks that could be interpreted as racist, sexist, or bigoted.

- Do not giggle or play with your hair during an interview.

- Do not fidget.

- Do not try to impress the interviewer with all the big words you know. Speak simply and your intelligence will be obvious.

- Do not use slang or profanity. Use your best grammar. Most jobs require good communication skills and this is a perfect opportunity to showcase yours.

Business Etiquette:
Minding Your Own Business

- Do not ask an interviewer to put in a good word with your prospective boss. It is not the interviewer's job to be your advocate.

- Do not ask any interviewer to relay a message to another. If you think it was nice to meet Mr. Smith, tell him yourself with an appropriate thank-you note.

> **It is estimated that as much as 85 percent of job success is based on "soft skills," that is, skills in dealing with people.**

- Do not trash former employers. No matter how bad your previous situation may have been, an interview is not the place to vent your frustration.

- Do not ask for inside information about the company or the job.

- Do not wear extreme clothing. Human resource professionals list the following as things you should never wear to an interview:

  - A backpack or fannypack
  - Earrings on men
  - Facial piercings
  - Fishnet, other patterned hosiery, or bare legs (no matter how tan you are)
  - Headphones around your neck
  - Heavy makeup (none at all for men)
  - Inappropriate footwear, including sneakers and sandals
  - More than one set of earrings on women
  - Overly bright or large-patterned clothing
  - Skirts that are too short

- Strong aftershaves or perfumes (some interviewers are allergic)
- Sunglasses on top of your head
- Telltale signs that you are wearing new clothes (make sure all tags have been clipped)
- Unnatural hair colors or styles

• Do not be surprised if you're asked to take a drug test. While this usually doesn't happen until a company is ready to hire you, your hiring will depend on your willingness to comply and whether or not you pass.

• Do not bring up salary, benefits, or perks; those topics are usually covered in a follow-up interview.

> **"Etiquette would not seem to play an important part in business, and yet no man can ever tell when its knowledge may be of advantage, or its lack may turn the scale against him."**
>
> Emily Post

What to Do

• Learn about the company ahead of time. What you know about your prospective employer during the interview can indicate your interest and your initiative. Here are some things that will be helpful:

- The proper pronunciation and spelling of the company's name
- What the company does
- The size of the company
- How long the company or division has been in business
- The general reputation
- Any stories about the company recently published

Business Etiquette:
Minding Your Own Business

- Confirm the time of your appointment ahead of time.

- Know ahead of time where you are going so you don't have to look for an address at the last minute and risk the chance of being late.

- Come prepared. Have extra copies of your resume with you. Also, have your reference list available in case it is requested.

- Have your papers well organized and available in a nice briefcase or portfolio.

- Wear clean, conservative, and well-pressed clothes that present a professional image.

- Extend your hand and introduce yourself upon meeting the person who will interview you.

It is said that when Henry Ford was hiring a new executive, he would take him to lunch to observe his behavior when the food was served. If the job candidate salted his food before tasting it, Ford wouldn't hire him, believing that this one action indicated a tendency to make hasty decisions without knowing all the facts first.

- Make eye contact with the interviewer.

- Wait to be asked to sit.

Business Etiquette:
Minding Your Own Business

- Keep your hands poised as you talk. Relaxing them will help keep you more relaxed overall.

- Know what an interviewer is likely to ask and be ready with possible answers. Common questions include "Tell me a little about yourself," "Why did you leave your last job?" And "What are some of your strengths and weaknesses?"

- Turn off your cell phone, pager, and anything else that might interrupt your interview.

- Be genuine, but not overly friendly, with the interviewer.

- Plan appropriate responses before answering questions. Be careful not to fill silences with nervous responses.

- Keep your responses positive.

- Ask questions that indicate your interest in the job. Some examples are as follows:

> **A thank-you note can make you stand out in the minds of your interviewers. Even if you don't get this job, your courtesy may put you in contention for another job later.**

  - What is a typical day like?
  - What training is required for this job?
  - What opportunities for advancement are there?
  - What are the challenges and rewards of this job?

- Thank the interviewer(s) for his, her, or their time before you leave.

- Send a thank-you note to each of your interviewers.

> In recent surveys, 80 percent of the respondents reported an increase of rudeness in business. Of that number, 58 percent said they would take their business elsewhere if treated rudely by employees.

- Ask about the next step if you are interested in the job. If you are not interested, politely thank the interviewer for taking time to speak with you, and leave on a positive note.

OFFICE BEHAVIOR

Nowhere is proper behavior more important than in your own office, with the people you work with every day. Like family members, co-workers often become slack in their attitudes toward each other, but efforts should be made to remember proper behavior.

> "I have a respect for manners as such, they are a way of dealing with people you don't agree with or like."
>
> Margaret Mead

What NOT to Do

- Do not loiter. Even if you don't have anything pressing to do, your presence might keep others from getting their work done.

- Do not gossip. Not only will you appear to be a busybody, but it will also seem that you spend more time working the grapevine than the job.

Business Etiquette:
Minding Your Own Business

- Do not put down co-workers, publicly or privately.

- Do not use company time for idle talk or chit-chat.

- Do not talk on your cell phone for extended periods during work hours.

- Do not keep visitors waiting beyond their appointment times. Their time is as important as yours. If an unavoidable delay occurs, apologize for the inconvenience.

- Do not use discriminating language.

- Do not open a co-worker's mail or listen in on his or her phone conversations.

> **The number one complaint about bosses by the people who work for them is that the workers are ignored until the boss gives them their first assignment of the day.**

- Do not try to claim credit not rightfully yours.

- Do not kiss or hug co-workers. Even in social situations where this might be acceptable, wait for the other person to make the first move.

- Do not engage in office romances.

- Do not worry about the rules of chivalry, which do not apply in business. The first one to a door goes through first. Hold it only to keep it from hitting the person behind you, or to help if that person is carrying packages.

Business Etiquette:
Minding Your Own Business

- Do not use first names until you are asked to do so.

- Do not monopolize office equipment such as the copier or the fax machine.

- Do not drink alcohol on the job, or have it at lunch when you will be going back to the office.

What to Do

- Greet people when you come in each day. It is rude not to acknowledge others when you first enter an office.

- Adhere to company dress codes.

- Keep your promises. If you say you'll stay late and help get a project finished, do it.

- Cultivate good phone manners.

- Return phone calls promptly.

- Answer correspondence as soon as you are able.

- Be punctual for all appointments.

> **It is estimated that 70 to 80 percent of today's business is done over the telephone.**

- Keep everyone involved in a project informed.

- Give credit where credit is due.

- Make reference to the team effort for any project. This also includes taking your share of the blame when things go wrong.

- Return borrowed items promptly and in good condition.

- Congratulate others on promotions and recognitions.

- Introduce your colleagues to office visitors.

- Remember to thank people when they help you.

TELEPHONE ETIQUETTE

Every time you make or receive a telephone call at work, you are representing yourself and your company. Make sure your voice and your manner indicate that you are a professional.

What NOT to Do

- Do not shout.

- Do not put a caller on hold without telling him or her first.

- Do not slam the phone down when you hang up or must step away for a moment.

- Do not take telephone calls when someone with an appointment is sitting in your office.

- Do not transfer a call to another person without telling the caller first.

- Do not be insulted if you're asked to leave a message or call back later.

- Do not chew gum or eat while talking on the phone.

> **When leaving a voice mail message, take advantage of the feature that allows you to play back your message after recording; you will be able to make sure your message is clear and communicates your needs.**

Business Etiquette:
Minding Your Own Business

What to Do

• Answer the phone with a simple "Hello," and identify yourself.

• Identify yourself and your company when you are the caller.

> **The outgoing message you leave on your voice mail is an important business tool. It should tell your name, your company or department, the date, whether you are in the office or not that day, when you will be back, and an alternate contact name while you are away.**

• State the purpose of your call and ask if you are calling at a convenient time. This will allow the other person the opportunity to speak with you when he or she has ample time to fully address your needs.

• Be honest about how long your call will take. Don't say "I'll be brief" if your call will really take longer than a few minutes.

• Be certain of the number you are dialing to avoid disturbing someone unnecessarily.

> **"Courtesies cannot be borrowed like snow shovels; you must have some of your own."**
> John Wanamaker

• If you reach a wrong number, it is important to say, "I'm sorry, I dialed the wrong number" before hanging up.

• Speak clearly and concisely when leaving a voice message.

Business Etiquette:
Minding Your Own Business

- Be sensitive to time pressures when you call busy people.

- When someone answers the phone, the caller should give his or her name before asking for the person desired.

- Express yourself clearly and concisely so you will be understood correctly.

- Hold the receiver so that you speak fully into it. Tucking it under your chin will keep you from being understood.

- Remember that the person on the other end of the phone cannot see your facial expressions and gestures to help facilitate your conversation.

In German business meetings, age takes precedence over youth. If you are in a group setting, the eldest person enters first.

- Always return calls. If you are unable to help the caller, direct them to someone who can.

- If you will be out of the office, have your voice mail message let callers know. Tell them when you'll be back in the office and when they can expect to hear from you.

- Make sure your voice mail system is working and receiving calls properly. An uncooperative answering system is the same as a rude person.

- If you need to leave the line for any reason, give the caller the option of waiting or being called back. If he or she chooses to wait, come back to the phone as soon as possible.

- End your call with "Goodbye," or an appropriate closing to signal the end of the conversation.

- Do your homework following the call. If you have promised to provide data, get the material to the other person promptly.

WORKING INTERNATIONALLY

The globalization of business makes it imperative that businesspeople know how to interact with international colleagues. Each country has its own ways of doing business that are mixtures of social and corporate norms; disregarding those, even unintentionally, can undermine critical business dealings. Pave the way for good relationships by being aware of sensitive issues in the countries you do business with.

What NOT to Do

- Do not refer to international business acquaintances by their first names unless asked to do so. Such familiarity is not as common in other countries as in the U.S.

> **If you are invited to someone's home in Kenya, do not bring flowers – they are used to express condolences.**

- Do not expect ideas about work to be the same as in the U.S. Many other cultures place more importance on time with family than overtime at work. Let your host be the one to suggest working extra hours.

- Do not use gestures that may be interpreted in undesirable or inappropriate ways, such as these examples:

Business Etiquette:
Minding Your Own Business

- Beckoning with a curled index finger
- Bowing
- Making eye contact – considered impolite in Asian countries
- OK sign – considered obscene in some cultures
- Patting the head – the top of the head is sacred in some countries
- Pointing or snapping fingers
- Standing too close or far away from others
- Thumbs up
- "V" for victory
- Waving your hand

- Do not take offense at actions that are merely reflections of a particular culture. For instance, North Americans may not engage in casual touching during conversations, but Latin Americans and southern Europeans do.

> **When conducting business with French companies, if you do not speak French, it is important that you apologize for not knowing their language.**

- Do not invade "personal space" when talking with co-workers without knowing their cultural preferences about this.

- Do not give gifts without checking to see what connotations are attached to particular gifts.

- Do not send flowers without checking to see how these will be interpreted. For instance, white flowers in China signify mourning. Red roses in Europe indicate romantic intentions.

Business Etiquette:
Minding Your Own Business

What to Do

- Know the official name of the country in which you are doing business. For example, Germany is actually the Federal Republic of Germany.

- Be familiar with basic facts about the country: its form of government, capital, and names of top government leaders.

- Offer your business card in an English version, as well as in the native language of the country.

- Make sure you know the right way to give someone your business card. In parts of the Middle East, you should never use your left hand to present your card; in many Asian countries, you always use both hands.

- Use titles offered by those you do business with. For example, if a business card identifies a business contact as "Doctor," even though it may be an academic designation as opposed to a medical degree, it is a faux pas not to use it in European countries.

> **In Japan, leaving your chopsticks in your rice is considered to be a bad omen.**

- Be aware of normal business hours and work days for the country with which you are working.

- Observe emphasis on rank and status. Different cultures place different values on age, gender, and levels of authority.

Business Etiquette:
Minding Your Own Business

- Be aware that fashion may signal your status and your respect for your company, as well as for the person with whom you are working. When in doubt, err on the side of conservatism and formality.

- Know customs about everyday logistics, such as how far in advance appointments should be made, and to what extent punctuality is stressed or ignored.

- Avoid jokes and stories that may not be received well in other cultures.

- Be aware of religious and cultural taboos and restrictions that should be considered when planning business meals.

Cell Phone Courtesy: Hazards of Secondhand Conversations

Cell Phone Courtesy:
Hazards of Secondhand Conversations

No modern device has been as helpful to as many people as the cell phone. And yet, is there anything more annoying than a cell phone ringing at an inopportune time, or an inconsiderate person talking too loudly on his phone in public? Signs that prohibit cell phone use in certain places may impose a measure of courtesy, but it is ultimately the responsibility of each individual to make sure that his or her use of this modern convenience does not inconvenience others.

What NOT to Do

- Do not be confrontational if someone nearby is being disruptive with his or her cell phone.

- Do not answer your cell phone while you are already interacting with someone in person. A ringing phone should not take priority over

In 2002, July was declared National Cell Phone Courtesy Month in an effort to eliminate rude behavior among the 137 million cell phone users in the U.S.

a flesh-and-blood person unless you suspect it is an emergency.

- Do not yell to accommodate static or a bad connection. Hang up and find a location with better reception to make your call.

- Do not talk about personal matters on your cell phone in public, especially relationships or personal medical news. Not only might you be overheard, but some transmissions can be received by others on their own phones elsewhere.

- Do not distract others with your conversation.

Cell Phone Courtesy:
Hazards of Secondhand Conversations

Most cowardly use of a cell phone? Over 1,000 guests were already waiting when the star striker of a Malaysian state soccer team called off the wedding in a cell phone text message to his bride-to-be. He was subsequently fired from the team for "tarnishing the state's image" by not showing up at his own wedding.

- Do not use your cell phone in places where use is prohibited. This is particularly critical in hospitals and on airplanes, where phone signals can interfere with proper operation of equipment.

- Do not cough or sneeze into the phone during a conversation. The noise of both of those is magnified on the other end.

- Do not use your cell phone while driving. Pull over if you must make or receive a call.

- Do not talk on a cell phone while paying at the grocery store or other service or retail establishment. If you can't end the conversation before getting in line, wait to check out after you finish the call.

What to Do
- Be familiar with your cell phone's features and how they can minimize inconvenience to those around you.

- Speak in a regular conversational tone when using your phone. People often tend to speak more loudly than normal when on a wireless call and don't recognize how distracting they can be to others.

- Keep your ringer simple. Although the variety of melodies and phrases offered as ringers is almost unlimited, no one wants to hear the latest pop tune or classical tidbit ten times a day.

- Play games discreetly. Noises from them can be annoying, so turn the volume down.

- Inform your companions in advance if you are expecting a call during a gathering or meeting, and excuse yourself from the room when you take the call.

- Use caller ID and voice mail to take your calls when you're in meetings, restaurants, or other busy areas. Not only will this be considerate to others, it will allow you to screen your calls and focus on the ones that are important.

- Set your phone to vibrate instead of ring if you must leave it on during meetings. This applies any time you are in public.

- Remove the earpiece when you are not talking on the phone. It is irritating for others who wonder whether you're talking to them or someone on the line.

- Use discretion when discussing private matters or certain business topics

> **A recently enacted law in Singapore says that drivers caught talking on a cell phone face not only stiff monetary penalties, but prison time as well after the first offense.**

in front of others. You never know who is within hearing range.

- Excuse yourself when talking on your cell phone. If you are in a public place, people will not want to hear details of your personal life. If you are in a meeting, your conversation will keep co-workers from continuing with their business.

- Use call waiting with discretion. Just because you can take another call doesn't mean you should. Give priority to the caller already on the line, and let your voice mail take a message unless the second call is urgent.

> **A recent survey shows that 60 percent of people think it's more unpleasant to sit next to someone talking on a cell phone in a movie theater than to visit the dentist.**

- Be aware that your phone will not only transmit your words, it will also send sounds around you. Be alert to music or crowd noises around you that could drown out your words. Public restrooms are the worst. You figure it out.

- Use text messaging. This silent service allows you to send and receive information without speaking on the phone.

- Practice wireless responsibility when driving.

- Watch where you are walking while using your cell phone. Don't bump into people on the street because you aren't paying attention.

Dating Do's and Don'ts: Conduct for Courting

Dating Do's and Don'ts:
Conduct for Courting

Whether you have known each other a short time or for a while, courtesy and respect are essential to a successful dating relationship. Simple considerations such as those listed below can help both parties enjoy time together. General guidelines are presented first and then some specifically for that most stressful of times, the first date!

What NOT to Do

- Do not keep your date waiting. Be ready when he or she arrives.

- Do not cancel a date without a legitimate reason.

- Do not complain if you are tired or don't feel well. If you really aren't up to the date, reschedule it.

- Do not make a scene in public if something goes wrong, such as poor service.

- Do not drink too much on a date.

- Do not be a nuisance by calling too often.

- Do not forget breath mints and cologne.

- Do not use jokes to camouflage anger over issues. Deal honestly with the thing that bothers you.

- Do not pay more attention to other people or things than you do to your date.

> **In Western countries in the 1800s, a young man could not speak to a young woman he knew until she had first acknowledged him.**

Dating Do's and Don'ts:
Conduct for Courting

- Do not say you'll call if you don't intend to.

- Do not discuss volatile issues like religion and politics in the early stages of a relationship.

- Do not lie about your marital status.

> **At a loss for words on a date? Ask open-ended questions about your date's job, family, or hometown.**

- Do not talk on your cell phone while you are with a date except in an emergency. A person on the other end of the phone should not take priority over someone you are actually with.

- Do not monopolize the conversation.

- Do not act possessive of your date.

What to Do

- Be sensitive to the other person's financial situation when making plans for which he or she is paying, or will be expected to contribute.

- Pay for the date when you do the asking.

- Call when you say you will.

- Make plans that will make your meetings enjoyable.

- Compliment your date about how he or she looks. People like to know that their efforts to look nice are appreciated.

- Let the other person know if you will be late.

Dating Do's and Don'ts:
Conduct for Courting

In seventeenth century Wales, ornately carved spoons, known as lovespoons, were made from a single piece of wood by a suitor to show his affection to his loved one. The decorative carvings had various meanings—an anchor might mean "I want to settle down," whereas a vine might indicate "love grows."

- Use your cell phone to smooth the way for your plans. Program in the numbers of places you'll be going in case you run late and need to call.

- Treat your date with respect.

- Guard personal details that you learn during your dating relationship.

A recent survey reports that in one month, there were approximately 40 million U.S. visitors to online dating sites. During one year, U.S. consumers spent $214 million on those sites.

- Be considerate of your significant other's schedule when making dates, and make sure to end your times together at a decent hour when you have important plans for the next day.

- Be honest if you decide that you do not want to continue the relationship.

FIRST DATES

The dreaded first date! It can be awkward, but can actually be enjoyable if you follow a few commonsense suggestions.

What NOT to Do

• Do not be late.

• Do not try to be someone you're not.

• Do not make a snap judgment about the other person.

• Do not send mixed signals. Forego the goodnight kiss that might be misleading if you really aren't interested in a second date.

• Do not give out too much personal information before you know the other person can be trusted.

• Do not be aggressive physically. Be sensitive to signals from your date.

• Do not promise a second date if you know you do not want one.

• Do not use foul language during your conversation.

• Do not talk about yourself too much.

> **One mobile phone company offers help to its customers stuck on a disastrous date: just dial SOS, hang up, and within minutes, they'll call you back with an excuse to leave. They'll even walk you through what to say to make your excuse believable.**

Dating Do's and Don'ts:
Conduct for Courting

- Do not go into details about your financial affairs.

- Do not talk about previous relationships that have failed.

- Do not monopolize the conversation.

- Do not bite your nails, scratch, or do other annoying personal things on your date.

> **Some of the best ideas for dates are the simple things you love to do— going to an art museum or riding bikes. Those everyday activities give the other person a chance to get to know you personally.**

- Do not smoke during dinner. Wait until the meal is over if you must have a cigarette.

- Do not treat someone you've just met as a potential mate. While it is true that most people eventually marry the people they date, don't start thinking about too much too soon. It could scare some people away.

- Do not take things so seriously. Have a sense of humor.

- Do not patronize your date. Be sincere.

- Do not wear out your welcome. Standing on your date's porch until 3:00 a.m. on your first date may be too much too soon. Find an appropriate time to end the date.

What to Do
- Confirm the date a few days beforehand.

Dating Do's and Don'ts: Conduct for Courting

- Get directions to your meeting place in advance and leave a little early.

- Plan your date for a public place so you will both be free to leave if you wish.

> **Courtship in the late 1800s frequently included the presence of a chaperone to ensure the woman's "purity." Parents would often sit in a room adjacent to where the couple was in order to monitor their conversation.**

- Consider going some place where you will be able to talk and get to know the other person as opposed to a movie or other activity where you will have to be quiet.

- Wear clothes that you like and that make you feel good; this will enhance your self-confidence.

- Turn off your cell phone. Give your date the attention he or she deserves.

- Take extra money just in case something unexpected comes up.

- Plan for the first date to be a short one, just in case things don't go well. If you hit it off, you can always extend your time together.

- Have a backup plan in case something goes wrong: weather changes, movies get sold out.

- Be a good listener.

- Try to draw the other person out of himself or herself.

Dating Do's and Don'ts: Conduct for Courting

- Make eye contact as you get to know each other.

- Ask questions to discover your date's interests.

- Keep the conversation current and relevant.

- Be truthful. Don't let your desire to look good lead you to create a false impression about anything.

- Try to have fun. It's just a date. The worst that can happen is that you'll spend an evening together and decide not to pursue the relationship.

- Bring breath mints. Dental floss is a good idea, too, just in case you get something stuck in your teeth during dinner (use it privately, of course).

- Be positive with your comments. If you've had a horrible day, keep it to yourself this time.

- Be safe. Just because a friend introduced you doesn't mean your date can be trusted. Be careful until you get to know each other.

> **Colonial suitors were guided primarily by practical matters: they could only marry when they were able to support a family with their income and possessions. Many believed that love developed only as a marriage progressed and not before.**

Disability Diplomacy: Encounters That Enable

Disability Diplomacy:
Encounters That Enable

*O*nly in recent years have we become enlightened enough to realize that there are considerate and respectful ways to interact with people with disabilities. The most important thing is to relax and realize that people with disabilities are just the same inside as other people. But in case you need them, here are some guidelines to help you with these encounters. General pointers are offered first, and then tips for dealing with specific types of disabilities.

What NOT to Do

- Do not ask personal questions about someone's disability. Be sensitive and show respect for his or her privacy.

- Do not use words like "invalid," "crippled," or "handicapped." Other unacceptable terms include the following:

  - Afflicted
  - Deaf and dumb
  - Defective
  - Deformed
  - Idiot
  - Imbecile
  - Moron
  - Normal
  - Not right
  - Retarded
  - Spastic
  - Suffering from
  - Vegetable
  - Victim of

Disability Diplomacy:
Encounters That Enable

- Do not refer to the disability as the person. For example, a person is not "an epileptic," but rather "a person who has epilepsy." If you are not sure what words are preferred, ask.

- Do not patronize people with disabilities.

> **The Americans with Disabilities Act of 1990 established "a clear and comprehensive prohibition of discrimination on the basis of disability."**

- Do not help without asking first if help is needed or wanted.

- Do not push or lean on a disabled person's wheelchair, cane, scooter, or crutches. They are part of his or her personal space.

- Do not pet or distract service animals.

- Do not call undue attention to the disability with exaggerated offers of help.

- Do not make assumptions. People with disabilities are the best judge of what they can or cannot do. If they are unable or do not wish to do something, they will let you know.

- Do not make decisions for people with disabilities. They would like to be included in the decision-making process.

- Do not stare at people with disabilities, especially if they have disfigurements. If you have children, make sure they know not to stare.

> **Guide Dogs for the Blind is a nonprofit, charitable organization that provides guide dogs and their training to visually impaired people in the U.S. and Canada. Dogs and services are free, thanks to the generosity and support of donors and volunteers.**

- Do not be embarrassed if you accidentally use idiomatic expressions that relate to the person's handicap, such as saying "I'll see you later" to a blind person. They often use such phrases themselves and usually do not take offense to them.

- Do not discourage children from asking questions about disabilities. Answer them simply and honestly.

- Do not ever use a handicapped parking space unless you are truly disabled.

What to Do

- Share social amenities, such as a handshake, as you would with other people; if the person with the disability is unable to reciprocate, he or she will tell you.

- Offer a smile with a spoken greeting if a handshake is not possible.

- Speak directly to the person with the disability, not just to the ones accompanying him or her.

- Be considerate of the extra time it might take for a person with a disability to do or say something.

Disability Diplomacy:
Encounters That Enable

- Offer assistance if you think it might be helpful, but if help is refused, do not insist.

- Respond to requests for help or accommodations with grace. Asking for help is not a complaint; it shows that the person with the disability feels comfortable enough to ask for what he or she needs.

> **If you serve food to a person who is blind, let him or her know where everything is on the plate according to a clock orientation— twelve o'clock is furthest from him or her, six o'clock is nearest.**

For those who are blind or sight-impaired

- Identify yourself and others who may be with you upon greeting the sight-impaired person. Try to indicate where you are all positioned in the room.

- Excuse yourself when you move away so the person is not left talking to an empty space.

- Offer your arm if assistance is needed; do not take theirs because people who are blind need their arms for balance.

- Walk on the side opposite of a guide dog if there is one.

- Give detailed descriptions of the setting as you walk together, noting any possible obstacles.

- Be specific in warning about a possible obstacle. Just saying, "Look out!" does not tell the person if he or she should stop, run, or step aside.

- Offer to read written information such as menus when needed.

- Place the person's hand on the back or arm of a chair you are offering.

- Count out change if you are involved in a monetary exchange with someone who is blind.

For those who are deaf or use a hearing aid

- Get the attention of a hearing-impaired person by tapping him or her on the shoulder before you speak.

- Follow the person's cues to know if he or she prefers sign language, gesturing, writing, or speaking.

- Look directly at the hearing-impaired person and speak clearly. Those who can read lips will rely on facial expressions and other body language to help understand you.

People who are hearing impaired make and receive telephone calls with a device called a TTY (teletypewriter), or a TDD (Telecommunications Device for the Deaf). Messages are typed onto the keyboard and transmitted over telephone lines. They are converted back to words when they reach the other party, and are printed out. When using a TDD service, be aware that they transmit everything, including background noises, and remarks you make to others.

Disability Diplomacy:
Encounters That Enable

- Be sure that large hats or glasses do not obscure your features.

- Keep your hands and food away from your mouth while you are speaking so that your mouth is not hidden from the lip reader.

- Be sure to be in adequate lighting for lip readers to see you clearly.

- Make sure your environment is free of distractions. Extraneous noises may create confusion if the hearing-impaired person can hear background sounds.

> **Mel Tillis became one of Nashville's most famous country singing stars despite his infamous speech impediment. He named his autobiography <u>Stutterin' Boy</u>.**

- Speak directly to a hearing-impaired person even when a sign language interpreter is present.

- Be sure the hearing-impaired person can still see your lips and follow the conversation even when you are speaking to others.

- Speak normally: shouting makes words less distinct and contorts lip movements.

- Talk a little more slowly than usual.

- Pause slightly when you begin a new topic.

- Let the hearing-impaired person know when you are leaving.

- Pay attention to your handwriting when you must write your message to be understood.

Disability Diplomacy: Encounters That Enable

- Watch for facial expressions that indicate a lack of understanding.

For those whose disability affects speech

- Listen attentively when talking to a person with a speech impairment.

- Let him or her know when you do not understand what he or she has said. Do not pretend to understand if you don't.

- Keep your manner encouraging rather than correcting.

- Ask short questions that require only short answers.

- Ask him or her to repeat words or phrases you do not understand. Offer the person a pen and paper to write the message, if necessary.

- Be sure to engage in conversations where writing will be possible if the speech impaired person relies on writing for communication. This will at least require writing supplies, a free hand, and some light.

- Nod now and then or interject words occasionally to let him or her know you are still listening and understanding.

- Participate in the conversation, allowing him or her a few moments to rest while you speak.

- Allow the speech-impaired person to finish what he or she is saying, even if he or she seems to be having trouble saying it. Don't finish sentences for him or her.

- Be sure that the speech impaired person really is finished speaking when you think he or she is.

Disability Diplomacy:
Encounters That Enable

For those with a learning- or brain-function disability

- Keep communication simple. Rephrase comments or questions as needed.

- Be patient when the person tries to tell or show you what he or she wants.

- Stay focused as he or she responds to you.

- Be prepared to write your communications if requested. Verbal messages sometimes get scrambled and can be processed better when presented on paper.

- Be aware of any distractions and noises that may hinder understanding.

- Be understanding of poor impulse control, or inappropriate comments or gestures. Remember that these are out of the person's control.

For those who use a wheelchair

- Put yourself at eye level when talking with someone in a wheelchair. Sit or kneel in front of the person if possible.

- Rearrange furniture or other objects as necessary to accommodate a wheelchair.

- Place as many items as possible within reach of the person in the wheelchair.

- Make sure ramps and wheelchair-accessible doors are unblocked and free of debris.

- Keep in mind that chairs with arms or higher seats are easier for some people to use; offer those when available.

E-mail Etiquette: Netiquette

E-mail Etiquette:
Netiquette

E-mail is now a common form of business and personal communication, dispersing information with amazing speed and scope. The technology may be relatively new, but old-fashioned courtesy is still the main guideline.

What NOT to Do

• Do not "shout"; in e-mail terms, don't use all capital letters. Caps may be used for occasional emphasis, but should not be used for entire texts.

• Do not "mumble," or type in all lower case letters.

• Do not send abusive, threatening, or distasteful messages.

• Do not send an e-mail when you're angry. This applies to personal e-mails, but especially to those in a business context. Damage control in the latter can be difficult.

> **The first e-mail was sent in late 1971 to announce its own creation. Included in the message were instructions on using the @ character in e-mail addresses.**

• Do not write anything personal that you wouldn't want others to read. After your e-mail leaves, you have no control over where it may go in addition to your intended recipient.

• Do not send a lengthy e-mail when you can express your message in just a few words. The longer the text, the less likely the recipient is to read it.

E-mail Etiquette:
Netiquette

- Do not leave your e-mail open and unattended; anyone could send out offensive or embarrassing messages in your name.

- Do not overuse priority and urgent indicators. If you "cry wolf" too often, people will not know when to take you seriously.

- Do not overdo attachments. Not only should you not send too many, but you also should not send very large ones without checking with the recipient first. Some e-mail providers place restrictions on the size of messages a user is able to receive. When someone sends a large attachment, the receiver may be locked out of his own mailbox.

> **"Good manners will open doors that the best education cannot."**
> Clarence Thomas

- Do not over-quote. Use only relevant portions of whatever you are reproducing.

- Do not forward forwarded messages to your friends and co-workers. Most people don't enjoy receiving chain letters via their e-mails.

- Do not send copies of e-mails to people unless they need to be copied. In addition to cluttering up their mailboxes, it can make them feel awkward, thinking they are responsible for doing something with the information.

- Do not send e-mails containing offensive remarks about religions, sexuality, or other sensitive topics.

What to Do
- Be brief. You're not writing a novel; you're writing something between a short note and a memo. If your reader receives a lot of e-

mails each day, he or she will welcome a concise one.

- Enter a subject heading. In today's climate of spam and viruses, an e-mail without a subject looks suspicious, and is likely to be deleted unread.

- Use a salutation before the text.

- Use plain text only. Not every e-mail program can interpret HTML.

- Keep current. Read and respond to your messages promptly.

- Identify yourself clearly. Do not assume that your recipient knows who you are by your return address.

- Review the original question when you give an answer. This provides a context for your comments.

- Treat e-mail confidentially. If somebody sends you information or ideas, do not assume that you have their permission to reproduce it. Unless you are explicitly told otherwise, always assume that e-mails you receive are for your eyes only.

> **Flames are online shouting matches, complete with insults and personal attacks. They are common on message boards.**

- Strip down extraneous information if you are forwarding an e-mail. It cuts down on the size of the message and makes it easier to read.

- Observe standard grammar and spelling guidelines. This is especially true if you are using e-mail for a business relationship, since misspelled and misused words will tarnish your professionalism. Your spell check will help you, but do not rely on it entirely: even spell check may not alert you to legitimate words used out of context.

- Add "Please" and "Thank you" to e-mail requests. The computer may not be human, but the person reading the message is, and politeness will count.

- Get your facts straight. People will notice if you send incorrect information, and will have the saved e-mail as proof of your blunder.

- Consider your words carefully. Your reader will not have the benefit of your facial expressions to understand your tone. Some users add "smiles" at the end of their text to help with this. Here are some examples, but be careful—their use is by no means universal.

:-)	Smiley face; happy.
:-D	Really happy.
;-)	Wink (light sarcasm).
:-(	Frown.
:-I	Indifference.
:-/	Perplexed.
:-O	Yell; I'm surprised.
:-p	Sticking your tongue out.
: -X	My lips are sealed.
:'-(	I'm crying.

E-mail Etiquette:
Netiquette

- Here are some abbreviations also commonly found in e-mails.

BTW	By the way.
FYA	For your amusement.
FYI	For your information.
FWIW	For what it's worth.
IMHO	In my humble opinion.
IOW	In other words.
OTOH	On the other hand.
ROTFL	Rolling on the floor laughing.
TTFN	Ta ta for now.
TTYL	Talk to you later.

- Be sure you and your reader mutually understand any abbreviations or acronyms you use. If you are unsure, use the abbreviations with an explanation immediately behind it in parentheses the first time it is used.

- Remember that all laws governing copyright, defamation, discrimination, and other forms of written communication also apply to e-mail.

- Use blank lines (hard carriage returns) to separate your paragraphs. This makes your message easier to read.

- Use spaces for indenting when necessary; tabs should be avoided because different e-mail programs show them differently onscreen.

- Limit signatures to four to six lines.

Eating Out: Don't Slurp or Burp!

Eating Out:
Don't Slurp or Burp!

*O*ur society is much more casual than in previous decades, but there are times when formal dining etiquette is essential. Here are some things you should be aware of during those times. If they sound familiar, they are—they're the good old basics that mom tried to tell you!

What NOT to Do

• Do not force your way to the front of a waiting line and try to bribe the hostess for a table. Tipping a maitre d' who has given you a good table is acceptable, but trying to buy a good table is out of line.

• Do not call your server "Honey," "Sweetie," or other terms of endearment.

• Do not snap your fingers to get the attention of your server.

> **Dining in Argentina? Hands should be kept on the table, not in the lap.**

• Do not snap open your napkin. When seated, place it quietly in your lap, not in your shirt.

• Do not salt or pepper your food before tasting it. To do so is an insult to the chef.

• Do not season a dish that everyone will share. Limit your creative additions to your own portions.

• Do not cut up your entire meal before you start to eat; cut a small portion, and then more as needed.

• Do not wipe off silverware when eating out. If you discover a utensil that is not clean, ask your server to replace it.

Eating Out:
Don't Slurp or Burp!

A belch in ancient society was a compliment to the cook, but in modern society it is considered to be rude. Another gesture of appreciation was the act of taking home leftover food—that's one we still enjoy!

- Do not eat with your fingers, unless you are eating a finger food.

- Do not talk with your mouth full.

- Do not pick at your teeth during dinner to remove food. Excuse yourself from the table and go to the restroom where you can remove the particle in private.

- Do not smoke at the table. Many restaurants now prohibit smoking anyway.

- Do not fill your mouth with too much food.

- Do not reach across people to get the salt and pepper, butter, etc. Ask the person nearest the items to pass them to you.

- Do not pick up dropped utensils. Ask your server to bring a replacement.

- Do not make a lot of fuss if you spill something. Take care of it as quietly as possible.

- Do not spit bad food or gristle into your napkin. Remove it with the same utensil it went in with. Place the piece of food on the edge of your plate and cover it with other food if possible.

Eating Out:
Don't Slurp or Burp!

- Do not slurp your soup from your spoon. Spoon the soup away from you when you take it out of the bowl and sip it from the side of the spoon. If the soup is too hot to eat, let it sit until it cools; do not blow on it.

- Do not blow on your coffee or drink it noisily.

- Do not leave the table during a meal. If you absolutely must go somewhere, be sure to excuse yourself first.

- Do not play with the table utensils or crumble the bread.

- Do not put your elbows or personal items on the table.

- Do not talk loudly or boisterously.

- Do not indicate if you see something unpleasant in the food. Handle it discretely.

- Do not lick your fingers.

- Do not apply cosmetics or comb your hair at the

> **In the eleventh century, people in Europe ate with their fingers. A well-bred person used only three fingers: the thumb, index, and middle.**

table. Some manners experts say it's ok to apply lipstick, but only if it's done quickly: don't apply liner, lipstick, and gloss.

- Do not spit out food that you discover is too hot. Reach for your water and take a quick swallow.

- Do not use or chew on a toothpick in public.

- Do not lean on the table, or backwards in your chair.

Eating Out:
Don't Slurp or Burp!

> **Why is it rude to have elbows on the table? When this rule originated, people squeezed into long tables with benches for seats, similar to a school cafeteria table. If you had elbows on the table, they were in the next person's plate!**

- Do not ask for a doggy bag when you are the guest. Save leftovers for more informal situations.

- Do not lean back and announce, "I'm through" when you have finished eating.

- Do not leave your spoon in your cup. It looks unattractive there, and could cause a spill.

- Do not wave your utensils around with food on them while you talk.

> **Children in the late nineteenth century ate in the kitchen until they learned proper and appropriate table manners; only then were they permitted to join the adults in the dining room.**

- Do not complain about service when you are a guest. If you must vent about poor service, send a letter to the manager of the restaurant the next day.

What to Do
- Take manageable bites.

- Eat as quietly as possible.

Eating Out:
Don't Slurp or Burp!

- Sit close enough to the table so each bite is brought to the mouth without having to lean forward. Sit straight without sitting stiffly.

- Summon your server by catching his or her eye and raising your hand, finger pointing up, as if to say "Attention." If you are unable to engage his or her attention, you may ask another server to call yours for you.

- Blot lipstick before eating so smudge marks are not left on glasses or cups.

- Eat only finger foods with your fingers, which include the following:

   Artichoke – The artichoke is the leaf-enclosed flower bud of a plant that is in the thistle family. It is usually served steamed with a dipping sauce. To eat it, pull a leaf off, dip it, scrape the flesh from the base of the leaf with your top teeth, and discard the leaf on the plate provided for that purpose. Continue eating the leaves until the prickly "choke" is revealed. Switch to fork and knife, first to remove the choke, then to eat the heart and base.

   Asparagus – Asparagus may be eaten with the fingers as long as it is not covered with sauce, or is not too mushy to pick up easily. Of course you may use a fork and knife if you prefer.

   Bacon – Bacon may be eaten with the fingers for a very practical reason: if you tried to cut it with a fork, it would probably shatter, and the pieces would then be nearly impossible to "round up" with your fork.

   Bread – Bread should always be broken, never cut with a knife. Tear off a piece no bigger than two bites and eat that before tearing off more. If butter is provided, butter the small piece just before eating it. Some experts advise putting a small amount of butter on your own bread plate before putting it on the bread. Then if you need more butter, get it from your own plate instead of going back to the common source.

Cherry Tomatoes

– Except when served in a salad or other dish, cherry tomatoes are eaten with the fingers. Remember that they squirt, so find one small enough to eat whole.

> **"Manners are a sensitive awareness of the feelings of others. If you have that awareness, you have good manners, no matter what fork you use."**
>
> Emily Post

Cookies – Unless cookies are broken into small pieces in your dessert, in which case you would eat them with a spoon, they are eaten with your fingers.

Chips, French Fries, Fried Chicken, and Hamburgers – These items won't be served at a formal dinner, but when you are served them, do eat them with your fingers unless they are so messy that they absolutely require a knife and fork.

Fruits and Berries on the Stem – Fruits on their stems are intended to be eaten with the fingers. When they are served in a bowl, use a spoon.

Eating Out:
Don't Slurp or Burp!

Hors d'oeuvres, Canapés, Crudités – Almost everything served at a cocktail party or during a pre-meal hour is intended to be eaten with the fingers. Even when these are served at a regular meal, they may be eaten with the fingers.

Pizza – Pizza is cut into manageable pieces and then picked up and eaten with the fingers.

Sandwiches – Unless they are open-faced, too tall to fit in the mouth, or saturated with sauces or mushy fillings, sandwiches are intended to be eaten with the fingers.

• Start with utensils on the outside, and work your way "in." You will normally find the following:

Salad fork – If a salad is served before the entrée, this smaller fork will be found to the left of the dinner fork. If salad is to be served after the entrée, as in some very formal meals, the salad fork will be to the right of the dinner fork.

Dinner fork – This is the largest fork; it is used to eat the entrée as well as side dishes.

> **When forks were first used in Tuscany around the eleventh century, they were condemned by the clergy, who believed that food was a gift from God and as such, only the human hand was fit to receive it.**

Eating Out:
Don't Slurp or Burp!

Soup spoon/fruit spoon – If soup or fruit is served as a first course, this spoon is the outer most utensil on the right side of the plate.

Dinner knife – This large knife is used for the entrée, and is found just to the right of the plate.

Butter knife – This small knife is placed across the edge of the bread plate. It is placed there each time after it is used to butter the bread.

Dessert fork/dessert spoon – These might be paired and placed above the dinner plate before the meal, or they might be brought to you with dessert.

> **"Nothing indicates a well bred man more than a proper mode of eating. A man may pass muster by dressing well, and may sustain himself tolerably in conversation; but if he be not perfectly 'au fait,' dinner will betray him."**
> **Hints on Etiquette, 1836**

- Encourage your dinner partners to eat before their food gets cold if their food arrives before yours.

- Reach for anything that does not necessitate stretching across your neighbor. For items out of your reach, simply ask others to pass what you need.

- Pass items to others if you are the closest one to the items. Do not help yourself to the item until the original requester has received it and taken what he or she wants.

- Simply say "No, thank you" to dishes that you dislike or are unable to eat. In very formal settings, take at least a little of every dish that is offered; you can then spread it out on your plate so it is barely noticeable that you have not eaten much.

- Pass the salt and pepper together when someone asks, even if they only ask for one of them.

- Say "Please" and "Thank you" when asking for and receiving items out of your reach. These basics never go out of style.

- Excuse yourself quietly by saying "Excuse me" to no one in particular if you burp, hiccup, or have other unfortunate accidents during the meal.

- Place your napkin on your chair if you leave the table during the meal.

- Pace yourself and try to finish at about the same time as everyone else.

- Place your knife and fork on the plate parallel to each other, with points facing away from you, when you are finished. When you are merely resting between bites, place them in the "X" position, with the fork bottom on the left, and the knife bottom on the right.

- Indicate that you are finished by leaving your napkin next to your plate. Note that this is never done until everyone is finished.

- Tuck waste paper from sugar packets and other items under the rim of your plate. These should not be put in the ashtray.

Eating Out:
Don't Slurp or Burp!

- Sip beverages when your mouth is empty and has been wiped with a napkin. The only exception is when your mouth has been burned, in which case you may take a drink with food in your mouth.

- Wait for all to finish before leaving the table.

- Remember to thank your host and/or hostess for a delicious meal.

Making a toast is a custom developed by knights who were afraid of being poisoned by their enemies. Clinking glasses together meant that whatever was in one drink (even poison), was passed into both glasses. That made it in the best interest of both parties to not let friends drink an "evil" drink.

Everyday Good Manners: Customs and Courtesies

Everyday Good Manners:
Customs and Courtesies

*E*very day we encounter people in a variety of situations. The way we meet and greet them creates lasting impressions. Here are some things to be sure to avoid, and then a list of things to do, which includes particular situations that we encounter every day.

What NOT to Do

• Do not ask people their age.

• Do not be boastful, arrogant, or loud in your conversations.

• Do not interrupt when others are speaking.

• Do not call people "Hon," "Dear," or other familiar terms unless you know them.

• Do not open a closed door until you have knocked and received permission to enter.

• Do not read other people's mail.

Covering your mouth when you yawn was begun for two practical reasons. The first was religious: it kept the Devil from reaching in and yanking your soul out of your open mouth during the yawn. The second was that in the Middle Ages, hygiene was not a priority. People covered their mouths to keep from swallowing one of the many flies that swarmed around them.

Everyday Good Manners:
Customs and Courtesies

- Do not wait to apologize if you have offended someone. Delaying will only make the situation worse.

- Do not overstay your invitation when you visit.

- Do not plan to stay overnight at a friend's home without being asked, or at least checking to see that it is convenient for your host/hostess.

> **It is common for everyone to speak simultaneously at Italian gatherings. This applies to business meetings as well as social events.**

What to Do

- Greet people when you meet them.

- Wait for a response after your greeting.

- Be yourself.

- Remember to say "Please" and "Thank you" when appropriate.

- Listen before speaking. Listening shows respect and indicates interest in others.

- Consider your words before you speak.

- Arrive on time when you have an appointment. Respect your time and others'.

- When seeing someone you've recently met, greet them and tell them your name, in case they don't remember. Add information about where you met, like, "Hey John, I'm Jane —we met at Sue's party."

One company has found a creative way to deal with people who talk during a movie: just hand the offender a "Shut Up" card. Resembling regular business cards, these come in packs of twenty and eliminate the need to "sh-h-h" those doing the talking.

As an audience member at a public performance

- Avoid colognes or perfumes that would be a problem for those allergic to them.

- Turn off your cell phone or pager during the performance.

- Leave your noisy jewelry at home.

- Wait until after the performance to talk. End your conversation at the first note of the overture.

- Make sure you do not hum or sing along with the music.

- Stay seated and do not leave the show while it is in progress unless there is an emergency.

- Make sure any children accompanying you behave properly.

Men tip their hats in recognition to those they meet, a custom that began when knights in armor lifted the visors of their helmets to show their faces.

- Unwrap candies and cough drops before the program begins.

Everyday Good Manners:
Customs and Courtesies

At an ATM

- Allow the person already using an ATM privacy for his or her transaction.

- Wait your turn by standing several feet away from the person using the ATM.

- Transact your own business quickly and do not keep others waiting.

- Keep your business simple. Go inside to handle detailed transactions.

In the supermarket

- Allow people in the checkout line with only a couple of items to go ahead of you if you have a full cart.

- Maneuver your shopping cart with consideration for others. Do not leave it unattended in the middle of an aisle.

- Replace your shopping cart in its proper place when you finish with it.

- Make sure your child behaves appropriately while you shop.

- Return items to their proper place if you decide you don't need them. This is especially important for refrigerated products.

> **In Chile, if you meet people you know and want to speak to them, you should kiss them on their right cheeks. If those people are with friends, you have to greet the friends with a kiss, too.**

Everyday Good Manners:
Customs and Courtesies

On the street

• Walk so you do not block other pedestrians.

• Put trash into garbage cans; do not throw it on the sidewalk or street.

• Respect public property and buildings—do not deface them.

• Pay attention to those around you when you use a cell phone as you walk.

When visiting patients in the hospital

• Wait to visit until you are sure the patient is well enough to have company.

• Keep your voice low when visiting so you don't disturb others.

• Make visits brief. No matter how much better the patient feels, visits may tire him or her.

• Wish the patient well without exaggerating. Don't tell the patient that he or she looks "great" when you both know it is not true yet.

• Call the patient's family for updates if the patient is not well enough to receive calls directly. Remember, though, that the family may not have time for lengthy conversations.

• Check to see if the patient has plenty of flowers before sending more. You may want to wait and send some when he or she goes home.

• Be selective about giving gifts of food. The patient may be on a restricted diet.

- Send reading material that is easy to read and upbeat.

- Select amusing and attractive get-well cards.

- Avoid talking about other people that have had the same condition. Each case is different.

- Respect the patient's privacy by not asking personal questions about his or her condition.

- Step out into the hall and allow the patient privacy if a doctor or nurse comes into the room.

With professionals who serve you

- Be considerate of the other person's time by keeping appointments promptly.

- Respect the person for his or her education and ability.

- Let the person know when service has been exceptional.

> **In Turkey, if someone raises his chin, shuts his eyes, and tilts his head back, he's not resting— this is the gesture for saying "No."**

- Avoid trying to get free professional advice in social situations.

With service people and salespeople

- Say hello, be congenial, and state what you want.

- Use the person's name if you know it.

- Communicate what you want in a clear manner.

- Be sure not to patronize those who help you.

- Thank the person for every service rendered, however small.

- Let a supervisor know when service has been exceptional, not just when it has been unsatisfactory.

With waiters and waitresses

- Give your server your attention when he or she comes to take your order.

- Use your server's name if you know it. Don't snap your fingers to get his or her attention.

- Be certain of your order before you place it, and do not change your order after giving it to your waiter.

- Inform your waiter quietly if something is wrong with your order.

> "It's nice to be important, but it's more important to be nice."
>
> John Cassis

- Tip your waiter or waitress an appropriate amount at the end of the meal.

INTRODUCTIONS

Introductions are required on many occasions, and yet people are often confused about how to go about making them. Here are some things to remember when helping people meet each other.

What NOT to Do

- Do not address significantly older people by their first names unless asked to do so.

- Do not address a business superior in a familiar way unless asked to do so.

Everyday Good Manners:
Customs and Courtesies

- Do not pretend to remember someone's name if you have forgotten it. Be honest and ask the person to refresh your memory.

- Do not forget to make introductions when you are in a group of several people. Even if you find that they already know each other, you should make the effort.

- Do not put your introduction in the form of a command: "Mr. White, shake hands with Mr. Whatley," sounds more like an order than a friendly gesture.

- Do not introduce your spouse in a formal way, such as "Mr. Bradford" or "Mrs. Fuller," unless you are speaking to a child. Refer to him or her as "my husband, Tony Baker" or "my wife, Peggy."

- Do not repeat names unnecessarily. It is cumbersome to say "Mr. Curtis, meet Mrs. Smith. Mrs. Smith, Mr. Curtis."

What to Do
- Introduce people using both their first and last names.

- Include any titles the person may have, such as Doctor.

- Make eye contact when introducing people.

- Include facts that others may find interesting, as well as descriptive words where appropriate, such as "my wife," or "my uncle" when introducing someone new.

- Introduce persons of lesser authority to persons of greater authority or age first.

- Introduce the younger or less prominent person to the older, regardless of the gender of the individuals. If there is a considerable age difference between the two, make introductions in deference to age, regardless of social rank: "Mr. Perkins, this is Josh, my son. Josh, this is Mr. Perkins."

- Always introduce a man to a woman: "Mrs. Johnson, I'd like you to meet Mr. Patterson."

- When introducing someone to a group, name the group members first. This has the practical benefit of not only providing their names to the individual, but

Handshakes originated when men began to present their empty hands to show that they were unarmed. A handshake meant they were going to talk instead of fight.

getting their attention for the introduction as well: "Jerry, Luke, and Kyle, I'd like to introduce Judy Snow. Judy, please meet Jerry Butler, Luke McDonald, and Kyle Jones."

- Introduce yourself if your host/hostess neglects introducing you to others.

- Pay attention when you are introduced to people. Use their name(s) again later to help you remember them.

- Ask how to spell a difficult name, or glance at the spelling on the person's business card.

- Connect a person's name to a common word that will help you remember it.

- Respond to informal introductions with a simple "Hello," or a short comment like, "I have heard of your wonderful work."

- Respond to formal introductions with "How do you do?" and the person's name.

> **The origins of today's etiquette began in the French royal courts in the 1600s and 1700s. Under King Louis XIV, a placard (the word "etiquette" means card or placard) was devised and posted with rules for all to follow.**

Flying the American Flag: Patriotic Protocol

Flying the American Flag:
Patriotic Protocol

The days following September 11, 2001, saw a dramatic revival of the spirit of patriotism. American flags were in such demand that none could be found in stores. Although this strong emotion has waned somewhat, many people still fly flags regularly, in particular on holidays, and should follow proper protocol when they do.

What NOT to Do

• Do not dip the flag to any person or thing.

• Do not fly the flag upside down unless you intend it as a distress signal.

• Do not use the flag as clothing, bedding, or drapery. You may, however, use red, white, and blue bunting as a covering for a speaker's platform, or for decoration in general.

> **The name "Old Glory" was given to the American flag on August 10, 1831, by Captain William Driver of the brig Charles Doggett.**

• Do not display or store the flag in any way that would make it easy to soil or damage.

• Do not place any mark, letter, or design on the flag.

• Do not use the flag as a receptacle for receiving, holding, or carrying anything.

• Do not use the flag for advertising purposes. Likewise, do not fasten advertising signs to a flag's staff.

Flying the American Flag:
Patriotic Protocol

> **Colors in the United States flag are symbolic: red is for valor, zeal, and fervency; white is for hope, purity, cleanliness of life, and rectitude of conduct; blue is for the color of heaven, for reverence of God, loyalty, sincerity, justice, and truth.**

- Do not use the flag as an element of a costume or athletic uniform. However, it may be worn on the uniform of military personnel, firemen, and members of patriotic or other national organizations.

- Do not allow any part of a flag to touch the ground. It should be received by waiting hands and arms when it is lowered.

What to Do
- Display the flag from sunrise to sunset on any day on which there is no danger that the weather will damage it. It is particularly appropriate to display the flag on national holidays and days of importance such as those listed below.

  - New Year's Day
  - Inauguration Day
  - Martin Luther King Jr.'s Birthday
  - Lincoln's Birthday
  - President's Day
  - Washington's Birthday
  - Easter Sunday
  - Army Day

Flying the American Flag:
Patriotic Protocol

- V-E Day
- Mother's Day
- Armed Forces Day
- Memorial Day (half staff until noon)
- Flag Day
- Father's Day
- Independence Day
- Labor Day
- V-J Day
- Constitution Day
- Columbus Day
- Presidential Election Days
- Veteran's Day
- Thanksgiving Day
- Pearl Harbor Day
- Christmas Day
- Election Days
- State and Local Holidays
- State Birthday

> **The United States flag was first authorized by Congress on June 14, 1777, which we now observe as Flag Day.**

- Flags may be displayed at night when they will be properly illuminated.

- Store the flag by folding it neatly and ceremoniously.

- Clean and mend the flag as necessary to keep it in excellent condition.

- Retire a flag when it is no longer fit to be displayed. It should be destroyed in a dignified manner, preferably by burning. Many

Flying the American Flag:
Patriotic Protocol

VFW and DAR groups hold ceremonies for this purpose and will collect flags needing to be retired.

- When the flag is displayed over the middle of the street, it should be suspended vertically with the union (stars) to the north in an east and west street, or to the east in a north and south street.

- When the flag is displayed with another flag against a wall with staffs crossed, it should be on its own right (the viewer's left), and its staff should be in front of the other flag's staff.

> **"We take the stars from heaven, the red from our mother country, separating it by white stripes, thus showing that we have separated from her, and the white stripes shall go down in posterity representing liberty."**
>
> George Washington

- When flown at half-staff, the flag should first be hoisted to the peak for an instant and then lowered to the half-staff position. The flag should be raised again to the peak before it is lowered for the day. Crepe streamers may be affixed to spear heads or flagstaffs in a parade only by order of the President of the United States.

- When state or city flags or pennants of societies are flown on the same halyard with the flag of the United States, the latter should always be at the peak.

- When other flags are flown from adjacent staffs, the flag of the United States should be hoisted first and lowered last. No other flag or pennant may be placed above or to the right of the United States flag.

- When the flag is suspended over a sidewalk from a rope extending from a house to a pole at the edge of the sidewalk, the flag should be hoisted out, union first, from the building.

- When the flag is displayed on a car, the staff shall be fixed firmly to the chassis or clamped to the right fender.

- When a flag is hung in a window where it is viewed from the street, place the union at the head and over the left shoulder.

- When a flag is displayed from a staff projecting horizontally from a building, the union of the flag should be placed at the peak of the staff unless the flag is at half-staff.

- When the flag is used to cover a casket, it should be placed so the union is at the head and over the left shoulder. The flag should not be lowered into the grave or allowed to touch the ground.

- When the flag is displayed other than by being flown from a staff, it should be displayed flat. If on a wall, the union should be uppermost and to the flag's own right (the viewer's left).

- When carried in a procession, the flag should be either on the marching right, the flag's own right, or, if there is a line of other flags, in front of the center of that line.

- When a number of flags and/or pennants are grouped together, the United States flag should be at the center and at the highest point of the group.

- When flags of two or more nations are displayed, they should be

Flying the American Flag:
Patriotic Protocol

flown from separate staffs of the same height. The flags should be of approximately equal size. International usage forbids the display of the flag of one nation above that of another nation in time of peace.

• When displayed from a staff in a church or public auditorium on or off podium, the United States flag should hold the prominent position, in front of the audience, and to the speaker's right as he faces the audience.

Funeral Finesse:
Final Formalities

Funeral Finesse:
Final Formalities

*F*ew of us are ever prepared for the loss of a friend or acquaintance. But dying is a part of living, and must be dealt with. There are many ways that friends and family can get through this difficult time.

FAMILY OF THE DECEASED

It has been said that the purpose for all the details that must be taken care of when someone dies is to give the grieving family focus and a purpose for getting through the first days of their loss. There are considerations to remember each step of the way, such as those listed below.

What NOT to Do

- Do not make more elaborate arrangements for your loved one than you are comfortable with. If you want a simple or a private service, especially if either was the wish of the deceased, indicate your intentions and plan accordingly.

- Do not succumb to pressure to spend more money than necessary for any service related to interment of your loved one.

> **An 1860s woman mourning her husband would have had no social activities for two-and-a-half years, during which time she would have worn nothing but black clothes. A husband mourning his wife, however, spent only three months in a black suit.**

Funeral Finesse:
Final Formalities

- Do not hesitate to ask questions about financial arrangements that are unclear.

- Do not be reluctant to ask for help with specific tasks during your time of loss. Most people will be glad to know of some way they can help.

- Do not sign papers unless you understand them completely.

> **Where did the word pallbearer come from? Pall was a fifteenth century word used to describe a cloth that covered a coffin, hearse, or tomb. The term pallbearer originally referred to those that held the corners of the pall cloth at a funeral. Eventually, those who carried the coffin itself came to be called pallbearers.**

- Do not expect more of yourself than you are able to do, physically or emotionally.

- Do not be impatient with yourself. Grieving is a process.

What to Do
- Notify other family members and close friends about the death.

- Contact the funeral home and schedule a time to meet to finalize arrangements.

- Be prepared to make decisions about such things as the following:

Funeral Finesse:
Final Formalities

- Type of service: funeral or memorial
- Time of service
- Place of service
- Music for the service
- Speakers to offer eulogies
- Cremation, interment, or entombment
- Pallbearers and honorary pallbearers
- Clergyman to be in charge of the service

> **"They say such nice things about people at their funerals that it makes me sad to realize that I'm going to miss mine by just a few days."**
>
> Garrison Keillor

- Gather photographs that may be displayed at visitation.

- Send handwritten thank-you notes as soon as you feel strong enough to do so. Be sure and include the following people:

  - The clergy who handled the services
  - Friends or relatives who helped direct or plan the proceedings
  - The honorary pallbearers and ushers
  - The people who gave eulogies
  - Those who sent telegrams, cards, flowers, food, or who gave charitable contributions in memory of the deceased

FRIENDS AND ACQUAINTANCES OF THE DECEASED

It is difficult to know what to do or say to help the grieving family during the loss of a loved one. The best you can do is to offer your sincere feelings, taking into account the things listed below.

What NOT to Do

• Do not say things to family members that will upset them. Avoid the following statements:

  – "At least he/she didn't suffer."
  – "Be strong!"
  – "Death was a blessing."
  – "I could never handle this like you are."
  – "I understand how you feel."
  – "It was God's will."
  – "It's all for the best."
  – "It's time you put it behind you now."
  – "Look on the bright side."
  – "Perhaps it was his/her time."
  – "Something good will come out of this."
  – "You'll feel worse before you feel better."
  – "You can have other children."
  – "You're still young. You can always remarry."
  – "You need to keep busy so you won't think about your loss."
  – "You'll get over this."

• Do not ask for details of the death.

• Do not question arrangements the family has made.

Funeral Finesse:
Final Formalities

- Do not attend a funeral if the family has indicated that it will be private.

- Do not send flowers for a Jewish funeral without knowing the wishes of the family. Conservative Jewish practices omit flowers, but some Reform customs allow them. Often the family will indicate some other way to honor the deceased.

> **The Museum of Funeral Customs was founded to educate the public about the history of the American funeral and mourning customs, and funerary art.**

- Do not send flowers to a Catholic church, where only a spray of flowers for the top of the casket is permitted, usually from the family. One other bouquet may be allowed at the altar, but no doubt those will be from a close relation as well.

What to Do

- Pay your respects by saying something from your heart. The simplest sentiments are often the most appreciated. These phrases may be helpful at this time:

  - "How are you doing?"
  - "I am praying for you."
  - "I'm here and want to listen."
  - "I'm so sorry."
  - "Is there anything I can do?"
  - "It was a pleasure to know your dad. He was a fine man."
  - "Please tell me what you are feeling."

- "Take all the time you need."
- "Thank you for sharing your feelings."
- "This must be hard for you."
- "We will always remember him/her."
- "You must really be hurting."

- Send flowers to the home of the bereaved, to the funeral home, to the church, or the grave site. The family will state its preference. Be sure the accompanying card contains your name and mailing address.

- Send a sympathy card as soon as you hear about the death if you are unable to

> **The custom of sending flowers to funerals came about during the nineteenth century. When burial was delayed for any reason, flowers helped to mask the odor of death.**

visit with the family personally. The following suggestions may help you write a note that will be of comfort to those who have experienced a loss.

- Imagine what you would want to hear if you had experienced the loss.
- Be brief. The bereaved family will not be up to reading a long note.
- Be personal. Mention the name of the deceased and a special characteristic of him or her that you will always cherish.
- Offer support. Most people would appreciate being told that they are in your prayers and thoughts.

Funeral Finesse:
Final Formalities

- Be specific in offering help. Suggest something in particular you can do to help.
- Be careful not to offer advice as to how they should manage their grief. Mourning is a personal process.
- Close with expressions of comfort. End your letter with an expression of comfort, sympathy, or affection, such as "Love," "With sympathy," or "Thinking of you."
- Include your complete name. This would be especially important if your relationship with the deceased does not include a relationship with his or her family.

• Telephone the family as soon as possible if you live out of town. Keep the call brief, since others will probably be trying to call. Also, family members may not be emotionally prepared for a lengthy conversation.

> **Doorways were wide during the Civil War era not to accommodate wide skirts, but so coffins could pass through with a pallbearer on each side.**

• Prepare food to help feed the extra family members present. Extra household items may also be helpful, such as bags of coffee, rolls of paper towels, and toilet tissue to help accommodate extra visitors during this time.

• A memorial gift is always appropriate, especially when the family has requested such a gift in lieu of flowers. Usually the family will specify a specific organization or charity.

Funeral Finesse:
Final Formalities

- Remember to provide the family's name and address to the charity so they can send proper notification. It is acceptable to mention your gift in a sympathy note without mentioning the amount of the gift.

- Mass cards may be sent to indicate that a Mass for the deceased has been arranged. The offering of prayers is a valued expression of sympathy to Catholic families.

- Continue to offer support to the family during the grieving period by writing or calling on a regular basis.

- Include the family of the deceased in your plans in the days following their loss; they will let you know when they are ready to participate.

> **Victorians did not fear death itself as much as they feared not being properly mourned.**

Gift Giving:
It Really Is the Thought
That Counts!

Gift Giving:
It Really Is the Thought that Counts!

Finding the right gift for the right occasion doesn't have to be difficult. Most people are happy to receive any gift that is from the heart. Keep the following thoughts in mind as you look for just the right thing!

What NOT to Do

- Do not recycle gifts. This is thoughtless, and they can come back to haunt you.

- Do not send cash gifts through the mail. If you want to send money, send a check or a gift card.

- Do not question how much someone spent on your gift. Their thoughtfulness is the most important thing.

- Do not spend more on a gift than your relationship with the recipient dictates. Spending too much could make for an uncomfortable situation.

- Do not give people gifts they probably already have. For example, someone working in a jewelry store might not appreciate jewelry as a gift.

From the 1500s through the early 1900s, children learned etiquette at school. They were advised on such points as the proper way of kneeling before their teachers, the value of remaining silent until spoken to, and using a dinner knife as a toothpick!

Gift Giving:
It Really Is the Thought that Counts!

- Do not be late with your gift. Have it ready for giving in time for the special occasion.

- Do not try to impress people with overly expensive gifts.

- Do not make a show of disappointment if the gift you receive is not what you would have wanted.

What to Do

- Think of the intended recipient and buy for his or her taste, not your own.

> **South African etiquette dictates that gifts are not presented with the left hand. Gift givers must use the right hand or both hands when offering gifts.**

- Smile and say "Thank you," no matter how much you may dislike a gift. A sincere show of appreciation is the only appropriate response.

- Let the giver of a monetary gift know how you might use the money.

- Be as diplomatic as humanly possible if a gift must be exchanged for something else.

- Talk privately with the giver if the gift is too expensive, too personal, or not suitable to the occasion or your relationship. Never discuss this in front of others.

- When giving a monetary gift, put it in an envelope, money card, or greeting card.

- Consider cultural and religious preferences of the intended recipient.

Gift Giving:
It Really Is the Thought that Counts!

- When buying a wedding gift, check to see if the couple has listed their preferences with a bridal registry. Knowing what they need can be a big help. If they have not registered, consider household items to be used in the couple's new home, a check, or a gift card.

- For anniversary presents, remember that there are customary gifts for each specific anniversary.

	Traditional	**Modern**
1st	Paper	Clocks
2nd	Cotton	China
3rd	Leather	Crystal, glass
4th	Books	Electrical appliances
5th	Wood, clocks	Silverware
6th	Candy, iron	Wood
7th	Copper, bronze, brass	Desk sets
8th	Electrical appliances	Linen, lace
9th	Pottery	Leather
10th	Tin, aluminum	Diamonds
11th	Steel	Fashion jewelry
12th	Silk, linen	Colored gems, pearls
13th	Lace	Textiles, furs
14th	Ivory	Gold jewelry
15th	Crystal	Watches
16th	Silver hollow ware	Silver hollow ware
17th	Furniture	Furniture
18th	Porcelain	Porcelain
19th	Bronze	Bronze
20th	China	Platinum
25th	Silver	Silver

Gift Giving:
It Really Is the Thought that Counts!

30th	Pearls	Diamonds
35th	Coral, jade	Jade
40th	Rubies	Rubies
45th	Sapphires	Sapphires
50th	Gold	Gold

- For birthday presents, gifts involving birthstones add a personal touch. Here is a list of birthstones by month:

January	Garnet
February	Amethyst
March	Bloodstone or aquamarine
April	Diamond
May	Emerald
June	Pearl or moonstone
July	Ruby
August	Sardonyx or peridot
September	Sapphire
October	Opal or tourmaline
November	Topaz
December	Turquoise or zircon

- For corporate gifts, check first to see if there are any policies about giving gifts in the office.

- For housewarming gifts, choose something that will be used in the new home. A plant, a welcome mat, or a gift card for items for the home make great gifts.

Gift Giving:
It Really Is the Thought that Counts!

In some Asian countries, clocks and handkerchiefs symbolize mourning and are not given as gifts.

Gym Dandies: Exercising Your Common Sense

Gym Dandies:
Exercising Your Common Sense

Even gyms that do not post actual lists of rules expect common courtesies such as these to be observed.

What NOT to Do

- Do not wear heavy perfumes or colognes. The mix of sweat and perfume produces an aroma that has been likened to an old-fashioned outhouse.

- Do not wear makeup. Although your intention may be to look your best even during a workout, the makeup may run as you begin to sweat. This is probably not the look you want to be remembered for, and the makeup may also clog pores and cause acne.

- Do not forget to wear deodorant. In fact, use extra. In the gym, body odor is considered air pollution.

- Do not expect conversation from others. Most people are looking to get in, go through their routine, and leave.

> **"Manners are one of the greatest engines of influence ever given to man."**
> Archbishop Richard Whately

- Do not primp, preen, or pose. The purpose of gym mirrors is to check your form, not to admire yourself.

- Do not walk in front of people trying to use the mirror to check their form.

- Do not treat the locker room like your own private bath. Routine grooming should be done at home, and not in sight of others in the locker room.

Gym Dandies:
Exercising Your Common Sense

- Do not take food to the weight room. Aside from the distracting smell, it is inappropriate and messy.

- Do not hover. If you are waiting for a piece of equipment, patiently wait your turn while giving the current user time to finish.

- Do not sing along with your Walkman or any music you may be listening to.

- Do not talk during a group activity, even in the back of the class, thinking you can't be heard. You can.

- Do not slam down weights. Slamming is noisy, and could be dangerous.

> **Three strikes and you're out! Patrons at one New York gym are cautioned not to make loud, piercing screams that accompany some members' workouts. They get three warnings, and are then asked to leave. So far, no one has had to go.**

- Do not make loud grunting noises as you work out. People won't be impressed.

- Do not offer unsolicited advice. If you see someone doing something that could cause an injury, approach him or her carefully and always be pleasant when trying to offer help.

- Do not use your cell phone in the gym. Some gyms even prohibit cells phones inside the building because so many phones also have cameras that could easily take unflattering pictures of others at inappropriate times.

Gym Dandies:
Exercising Your Common Sense

- Do not use the drinking fountain as a place to spit or leave your gum. Also, if there is a line at the fountain, don't take time to fill your two-liter water bottle.

- Do not try to compete with the person next to you. Think about your own routine and your own results.

- Do not stare at other people regardless of what they are doing or wearing. Focus on yourself.

- Do not wear clothes that advertise another gym.

- Do not leave your personal items on a machine that you're not using. Even if you plan to use the equipment soon, you can't stake a claim for future use.

- Do not lose all inhibitions in the locker room. People may be embarrassed for you by your lack of modesty.

What to Do

- Be quiet. People are concentrating and do not appreciate distractions from the focus they need to achieve their fitness goals.

- Clean off the machines. You don't want to sit in someone else's sweat, why should they sit in yours? Covering seats or benches with a towel helps avoid this problem, and can keep germs from being passed through sweat as well.

- Share the equipment. If you are circuit training, trade off sets with someone else. You can rest while he or she uses the equipment.

- Wait until others are finished with their reps before asking for equipment that you need. Asking during a series interrupts concentration.

Gym Dandies:
Exercising Your Common Sense

- Remove heavy weights that you have used when you are finished so others do not have to do it.

- Abide by time limits set for equipment.

- Wear proper attire. Surveys have shown that few people appreciate scanty gym outfits. Think functional.

- Complete your outfit with appropriate gym shoes. "Outdoor shoes" bring in dirt that ends up on the floor, as well as in the machinery.

- Wash your gym clothes often to avoid odor.

- Pick up after yourself in the locker room. Your mother isn't coming to do this for you.

> **When asked why they don't go to the gym, one in ten of the respondents said it is because other gym members are "too rude."**

Tipping With Tact: Guidelines for Gratuities

Tipping With Tact:
Guidelines for Gratuities

Most people in the service industry depend on tips to
supplement their salaries. Tips are customary in our
society to show gratitude for services performed by other
people, but many people are unsure of just how much is
appropriate. The following guidelines will help with this
common dilemma.

What NOT to Do

• Do not routinely tip $1 and think it is sufficient. It is usually not.

• Do not routinely tip only your leftover coins. Anything under $1 is
considered leftover coins, except in a tip cup, or for small items,
like a cup of coffee.

• Do not feel you have to mention
the tip to the person you are
leaving it for. Everyone knows it
is expected.

• Do not withhold tipping in an
effort to send a message about
a particular service. You should
speak up instead. When you
don't say anything, no one
knows there's a problem.

> **Are tips based on
> the pre-tax or post-
> tax amount? Tips
> may be calculated
> on the pre-tax
> amount, but most
> people just use the
> whole bill.**

What to Do

• Here are some general suggested amounts to help you show your
appreciation to people who help you in various situations.

Tipping With Tact:
Guidelines for Gratuities

At the airport

- Charter pilot – nothing unless they provide extra services
- Electric cart driver – $2-3 a person
- Flight attendant – nothing
- Porter or skycap – $2 or more per bag for heavy bags; $2 extra for curbside check-in is optional. If you arrive late and he helps you get to your flight on time, tip an extra $5-20.
- Wheelchair assistant – $5 for a short distance, plus $1-2 per bag if he helps with luggage; $10-20 for a long distance, plus extra for luggage

At a hotel

- Bellman – $1-2 per bag when he shows you to your room. Tip again when you check out.
- Concierge – $5-10 for help with hard-to-get reservations or tickets. Tipping can be done at the end of the trip, or at the time of service.
- Doorman – $1-2 for hailing a cab; $0.50-1 for helping with your bags; $1-2 per bag if he carries them to your room.
- Housekeeper service – $1-3 per day; tip daily because there might be a different housekeeper each day. Leave the tip on your pillow. Tip on the last day also.

No tip is expected in restaurants in Italy, but you are charged a cover charge, and may be asked to pay for usually free items like bread. You may leave some coins on the table as you leave if you wish.

Tipping With Tact:
Guidelines for Gratuities

- Room service – 1-20 percent of the total charge; if gratuity is included, add nothing or $1
- Swimming pool or gym attendant – nothing, unless you require special services; then it is $2-5

Barbers, salons, and spas

- Barber – $2-3
- Hair stylist or color specialist – 10-20 percent
- Manicure or facial technician – 15 percent
- Massage therapist – 10-15 percent unless this occurs at a doctor's office, then nothing.
- Salon or spa package – 10-20 percent split among the service providers.

Delivery people

- Flower deliveries – $2-5 for normal deliveries; $5-10 for large ones
- Furniture/appliance deliveries – $5-10 per person; $20 per person for a large delivery
- Grocery deliveries – usually included in the fee
- Pizza deliveries – 15 percent, but not less than $2
- UPS/FedEx – nothing

Emergency roadside service

- Jump start – $3-5
- Tire change – $4-5
- Towing service – $5-20
- Unlock car – $5-10

Ground transportation

- Taxi, limo, paid shuttle, or van driver – 15 percent of the total fare; up to 20 percent if the driver helps with bags or makes

extra stops.
- Driver of courtesy shuttle – $1-2 per bag if he helps with the bags.

Holiday extras
- Apartment building superintendent – $20-100
- Baby sitter – two or three night's pay, plus maybe a gift
- Day care service – $25-70 plus a gift
- Doorman/concierge – $50-100 or more, depending upon building
- Garbage collector(s) – $15-20 each
- Hairdresser/stylist – $15 or more
- Housekeeper – one week's pay
- Mail carrier – $10-20
- Manicurist/pedicurist – $15 or more
- Massage therapist – $15 or more
- Nanny (fulltime) – one week's pay
- Newspaper delivery boy – daily: $25-50; weekend: $10
- Parking attendant – $10-20
- Personal trainer – $60-100 upon reaching goal
- Shampoo technician – $10

> **Tourists visiting Iceland will be glad to know that tipping in a restaurant is considered to be an insult!**

Movers
- One mover – $10-20 for a small move; $20-50 for an extensive move
- Multiple movers – $15-40 per mover, given to the supervisor for distribution

> **It is said that upon entering his favorite eighteenth century coffee shop, Dr. Samuel Johnson would drop a few coins in a box labeled "To Insure Promptness" (the initials of which are, coincidentally, TIP) in order to encourage more enthusiastic service.**

Restaurants or bars

- Bartender – 15-20 percent or $1 per drink. Settle up with the bartender before you go to your table.
- Coat check – $1
- Cocktail server – 15-20 percent of your bill
- Coffee shop – 10 percent of your bill
- Food server – 15-20 percent of the total bill
- Maitre d' – nothing, unless he gets you a special table or the restaurant is full and you had no reservation; then, $5-10 or more
- Musician in lounge – $1-5
- Musician that visits table – $2-3 for a special request; optional if he just stops by and plays
- Restroom attendant – $1
- Separate checks – 18 percent added to each check
- Table bussers – nothing unless they do something extra like cleaning up a spill; then, $1-2
- Wine steward – 10 percent of the wine bill

Wedding Wisdom: Tying the Knot Properly

*T*HE question has been asked and answered, and now there will be a wedding. Whether you are simply a guest, or the happy couple, there are things to do that can help make the big day and all the related events even more special.

BRIDAL SHOWERS

A bridal shower is a gathering of friends to celebrate an impending marriage. It is usually an informal occasion, but there is still a need observe certain courtesies.

What NOT to Do

• Do not invite anyone to a shower who is not invited to the wedding.

• Do not invite the same guests to multiple showers.

• Do not feel obliged to offer entertainment—opening the gifts is the main attraction. However, games may be played, and prizes awarded to guests.

• Do not feel compelled to send a gift if you are unable to accept the shower invitation.

• Do not include a registry list in the invitations. Guests may call the hostess and ask where the couple is registered.

> **The number of marriages in the U.S. has averaged 2.25-2.4 million every year for the past twenty years.**

• Do not spend more than you are able to on a gift. Two or more guests may join together to buy more expensive items.

Wedding Wisdom:
Tying the Knot Properly

What to Do

- Schedule the shower for two weeks to two months prior to the wedding.

- Consult the bride-to-be about the guest list unless the shower is to be a surprise.

> The first wedding shower was said to have taken place in the Netherlands in the eighteenth-century, when a bride's father refused to give her a dowry because he did not care for her choice of a husband. The groom shared his plight with the townspeople, who gave the couple enough of their wares and riches to make the marriage possible. The father was so impressed by the neighbors' "shower" of gifts that he consented to the marriage.

- Invite friends by sending informal, fill-in shower invitations, or by sending personal notes.

- Include the name of the guest of honor and the type of gift appropriate (linen, kitchen) on invitations. For lingerie showers, include the bride's sizes. Include color preferences of the bride and groom for household gifts.

- Greet guests as they arrive.

- Make sure all guests know each other.

- Send thank-you notes if the giver is not present at the shower to be thanked personally. In some communities, it is customary to send thank-you notes even if you have thanked the giver personally.

- Send thank-you notes to the hostess(es) for having planned the shower.

PLANNING A WEDDING

Your wedding is a special milestone in your life and you deserve to have it be the way you have always dreamed it would. Include these ideas as you start to think about your plans.

What NOT to Do

- Do not trade away your future by spending so much on the wedding that you enter your new marriage heavily in debt.

- Do not be afraid to tell people what you want. Be specific with wedding vendors about your plans. If you don't describe in detail the cake you want, don't be surprised if you show up at the reception and find a very different cake than you wanted.

- Do not wait until the last minute to handle details.

- Do not be swayed by other people's suggestions unless you truly like the ideas.

> **Juno is the goddess who rules over marriage, the hearth, and childbirth. The month of June takes its name from her, making it a common choice for weddings.**

- Don't focus so much on expecting perfection in details that you forget this is about the start of a marriage, not just a wedding.

- Do not register for the same things at different stores.

In 1228, Scottish women gained the right to propose marriage, a legal right that then spread slowly through Europe.

- Do not register for things you know you will never use. Only include items you really need.

- Do not overlook logistical needs of your attendants. Help with transportation and lodging information.

- Do not use wedding gifts until after the wedding.

- Do not send preprinted thank-you cards, which imply that the person receiving the note wasn't worth the time it would take to write the note by hand.

- Do not send thank-yous for several different presents in one card. For instance, if you have received a gift from Aunt Betty at a

The custom of the groom and bride not seeing each other before their ceremony on the day of the wedding stems from the days when marriages were arranged. There was the chance that the groom might see the bride and bolt—so it was safer for them to meet for the first time at the altar.

shower, and then later a gift at the wedding from the same Aunt Betty, you must acknowledge each in separate cards.

- Do not forget to put your new return address on all thank-you cards. Recipients will appreciate having your new address.

- Do not underestimate the time it will take to get your invitations printed and ready to be mailed six to eight weeks before the wedding.

- Do not include a list of places where the bride and groom are registered or a checklist of desirable and undesirable gifts. Guests can get that information from family members.

- Do not indicate "No Gifts" on the invitation. Many people prefer not to receive gifts in the event of a second marriage, or with an older bride and groom that already have established homes. Family members can share the request of no gifts, or can offer the name of a charity to which guests may contribute in lieu of a wedding gift.

> **Wedding and engagement rings are worn on the fourth finger of the left hand because ancient Egyptians thought that the "vein of love" ran from this finger directly to the heart.**

- Do not print "No Children" on the invitation. The way an invitation is addressed, by inclusion of some names and omission of others, will indicate who is invited.

Wedding Wisdom:
Tying the Knot Properly

- Do not put invitations on display on a bulletin board, or any public place which would indicate that each person reading it is welcome to attend, and could possibly bring another guest with them.

- Do not use labels to address wedding invitations. Every invitation should be addressed by hand.

- Do not feel guilty about the people you had to exclude from your guest list.

- Do not forget that your plans are about more than just a ceremony that will last a short while: it is about a marriage to last a lifetime. Use this time to lay the groundwork for good relations between families of the bride and groom by including both sides in the wedding plans, discussing what you will each call your new in-laws, and making opportunities for families to get better acquainted.

> **A word about the bride:**
> **"She must not swing her arms as though they were dangling ropes; she must not switch herself this way and that; she must not shout; and she must not, while wearing her bridal veil, smoke a cigarette."**
> Emily Post

What to Do

- Register for items in a variety of price ranges to accommodate guests.

- Go the extra mile for elderly or frail guests. Arrange to have them picked up for the wedding if necessary.

Wedding Wisdom:
Tying the Knot Properly

- Order extra invitations to allow for errors in addressing them.

- Make notes as soon as replies are received to help with seating when finalizing your table arrangements.

- Check postage. Be sure that you know the current cost of sending the invitations so that they are not returned for insufficient postage.

- Double-check spelling and proper wording for names of places that will be on the invitation.

> **The tradition of bridesmaids dressing alike and in the same style as the bride comes from a time when people believed that doing so would make it more difficult for evil spirits to pick out the bride and put a hex on her.**

- Use correct titles for names on the invitation list.

- Prepare the list with care. Although you may have to limit the number of invitations you send, your list should include the following people:

    - Immediate families of bride and groom
    - Attendants
    - Spouses or dates of the attendants
    - Grandparents of bride and groom
    - Clergyman
    - Distant relatives and work acquaintances, if possible

- Hand-stamp the invitations before mailing them; hand write or blind-emboss the return address.

- Send thank-you notes in a timely manner. Shower gifts should be acknowledged within ten days of the party and wedding gifts within two weeks after returning from the honeymoon. Wedding gifts that arrive before the wedding should be acknowledged immediately. In any case, all thank-yous should be done within three months of the wedding.

> **About fifteen percent of couples planning to say "I Do" decide "I Don't" before the wedding day. It's not always cold feet to blame: often there are reasons beyond anyone's control, such as illness and military service.**

- When acknowledging a gift from a group, a personal note should be sent to each person if the group is fewer than ten in number. If more than ten have participated, such as a gift from co-workers, one note, placed on a bulletin board is acceptable.

WHAT IF THE WEDDING IS CANCELED?

There is a saying that it is "better to be single than to wish you were." Doubts and last minute jitters are common. After all, there are few decisions in life so important and of such lasting consequence as choosing a mate. But occasionally, those jitters may turn into a decision not to proceed. If that happens, consider the following:

Wedding Wisdom:
Tying the Knot Properly

What NOT to Do

• Do not hesitate to call off the wedding just because people are already expecting it, and deposits have been paid.

• Do not worry what people will think. It's your life.

• Don't speak poorly of your ex.

• Do not fax or e-mail cancellation or postponement notices.

• Do not talk casually about details of the cancellation. Any conversation about it should indicate that it was a mutual decision made by both parties.

What to Do

• Let guests know about the change with printed cards, personal notes, or even by phone if there's not much time. Specific reasons for calling the wedding off need not be included unless those reasons are a family death or illness.

> **Contrary to what the movies portray, weddings are not frequently called off after wedding guests are already at the church. Most are called off two weeks or more before the wedding.**

• Let out-of-town guests know first so they can change or cancel their travel and lodging arrangements.

• Return the engagement ring! The couple should also return to each other any valuable presents that may have been exchanged.

- Return all the gifts (unused, of course) with a brief explanation.

- If you're only postponing the wedding, send another invitation with the new date when plans are finalized.

WHEN YOU ARE A GUEST

When you are a guest at a wedding, certain behaviors are expected, including these listed below.

What NOT to Do

- Do not assume that the couple knows you're coming to their wedding or not. You must send back your reply card before the date indicated.

- Do not bring extra people with you. The invitation is only for those specified on the invitation.

- Do not bring children if they were not invited. Some couples prefer not to include children.

- Do not feel that you must send a gift if you are not able to attend the wedding.

- Do not wear anything that could be considered to compete with bridal attire.

- Do not take offense if plans for special seating do not include you, even if you are a family member. Now is not the time to be petty, and this occasion is not about you.

- Do not talk during the ceremony.

"Something old, something new, something borrowed, something blue and a silver sixpence in your shoe." Something old refers to an item that represents a link with the bride's family and her old life. Wearing something new represents good fortune and success in the bride's new life. Wearing something borrowed, which has already been worn by a happy bride at her wedding, is meant to bring good luck to the marriage. Wearing something blue dates back to biblical times when the color blue was considered to represent purity and fidelity.

- Do not feel that you must participate in the religious rituals of the ceremony if you are of a different faith. Participate only if you want to.

- Do not distract others during parts of the ceremony in which you do not participate, such as certain religious rituals.

- Do not monopolize the bride and groom at the reception.

- Do not alter place cards or switch tables at the reception. They were placed a certain way for a reason.

- Do not indulge in too much alcohol if it is offered at the reception.

- Do not use the occasion to stir up old grievances or disagreements. The focus should remain the bride and groom.

- Do not take home doggy bags.

What to Do

- Send an RSVP as soon as possible, especially if you will be unable to attend.

- Respect the names on the invitation. Only those people whose names are there should attend.

- If you arrive at the church during the procession, wait until the bride has gone down the aisle before entering.

- If you are late for the ceremony, walk down an outside aisle to enter and find a seat quickly and quietly.

- Be on your best behavior.

- Pay for your own transportation and lodgings.

- Buy the couple a gift, something they can both use.

- Turn off your cell phone during the ceremony.

> **Today's honeymoon is a far cry from its beginnings, when brides were abducted and hidden for a period. Friends kept the whereabouts of the couple unknown until the bride's family gave up their search for her, and the couple returned.**

- Get permission before you make pictures during the ceremony. You may interfere with a professional videographer or photographer hired by the couple.

WHO PAYS FOR WHAT?

Deciding who will pay for what is an important first step to establishing your wedding budget. There are no longer rigid lines drawn about who will be responsible for which expense, so you won't see a list of what not to do. But if you need a place to start, here is a list of who traditionally pays for what.

Bride's family

- Bridal brunch
- Bridesmaids' luncheon
- Church fees
- Decorative items for the church and reception
- Flowers for church, bridesmaids, and reception
- Gifts for bridal party
- Groom's gift
- Groom's ring
- Janitorial workers
- Lodging for bridesmaids, if necessary
- Lodging for out-of-town guests

Placing a silver sixpence in the bride's left shoe is a symbol of wealth. This is not just to bring the bride financial wealth but also a wealth of happiness and joy throughout her married life.

Wedding Wisdom:
Tying the Knot Properly

- Musician fees for the ceremony and reception
- Printed items such as invitations, programs, napkins, and wedding novelties
- Reception costs
- Rice bags
- Wedding breakfast
- Wedding cake
- Wedding gown, headpiece, and accessories
- Wedding photos and videos

Groom's family
- Bride's bouquet
- Bride's gift
- Bride's ring
- Boutonnieres for groomsmen and ushers
- Clergy fees
- Gifts for groomsmen
- Groom's cake
- Honeymoon arrangements
- Limousine service for the bride and groom
- Lodging for groomsmen, if necessary
- Marriage license

- Mothers' corsages

- Rehearsal dinner

Bridal party
- Bridesmaid dress

- Gift for the couple

- The shower

- Transportation

Groomsmen
- Bachelor Party

- Gift for the couple

- Tuxedo or suit

- Transportation

There are a couple of thoughts about the origin of the wedding veil. One is that it is a relic of the days when a groom would throw a blanket over the head of the woman of his choice when he captured her and carted her off. Another is that during the times of arranged marriages, the bride's face was covered until after the wedding, when it was too late for the groom to run!

If You Liked *What NOT to Do in Polite Company!*, You'll Enjoy Other Books in This Series

What Not to Say! is a guide to words and phrases that are often mispronounced, misspelled, and misused. It sheds light on the differences between dozens of words that look and even sound similar, like *affect* and *effect*, and clears up questions about such phrases as "I could care less," and "if I was/if I were."

Plus, this small volume will help avoid redundancies and correct the most common style and usage problems. It even includes quotes from famous people that have been guilty of the same language mistakes the rest of us make.

What NOT to Say! is sure to be an indispensable tool for speaking and writing correctly.

ISBN:1-58173-360-7
$7.95

ISBN:1-58173-318-6
$7.95

What Not to Name Your Baby! can help you avoid making a mistake that your child will have to live with for a lifetime. It will let you know which names lend themselves to unfortunate nicknames, names with bad historical connotations, and even unusual names your favorite celebrities have chosen for their own children.

From unfortunate origins to names of serial killers, and those that are just plain ridiculous, this book will warn you away from potentially bad choices for your child.

Choose a name for your child that will be a blessing instead of a burden with the help of *What NOT to Name Your Baby!*